To David,
with best wishes

BLACK JACKS, FRUIT SALADS, CRICKET STUMPS ON THE WALL

BRIAN WATSON
PHOTOGRAPHY BY BREAD & SHUTTER

Book Guild Publishing
Sussex, England

First published in Great Britain in 2011 by
The Book Guild Ltd
Pavilion View
19 New Road
Brighton, BN1 1UF

Printed in Spain under the supervision of
MRM Graphics Ltd, Winslow, Bucks

A catalogue record for this book is available from
The British Library.

ISBN 978 1 84624 656 2

DEDICATED TO 'THE FEW',
THE BATTLE OF BRITAIN PILOTS
WHO GAVE UP EVERYTHING
FOR THE REST OF US.

To grow up in the 1950s was a wonderfully exhilarating experience.

A time of real austerity, yet such a happy time. As the clouds of war were finally blown away, it was a time of un-rationed laughter.

A time of pure excitement. For the first time in many, many years there was a future; a future that you could feel, see and smell.

The 'all clear' had finally been sounded, the blackout curtains had been drawn back for good. It was on with the demob suit, ready to blow the froth off the top of an inviting glass of stout.

This is a light-hearted look at that moment in time, as seen through the eyes of a young boy growing up in London, just a stone's throw from the famous Lambeth Walk.

If you were around at the time, this verse will make you smile, then that smile will grow to become the echo of the fun these words will inspire you to remember so fondly.

As the BBC's *Listen With Mother* presenters used to say, 'Are you sitting comfortably? Then we will begin.'

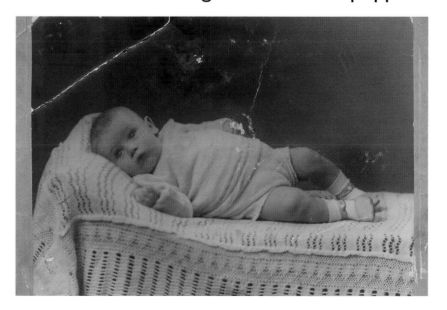

Sixty years ago next Thursday to be quite exact,
My dear mum was lying flat on her back.
T'was the early hours of the morning
When she gave out a shout,
The nurses came running and look what popped out.

Being brought up in London after World War Two,
Gave me and my mates plenty to do.
There were bombsites and tin hats and shelters galore,
All great for hiding and playing at war.
The one thing that's funny and I know you'll agree,
Who always played Hitler? Of course it was me.

A childhood in the fifties, Jamboree bags and all,
Black Jacks, Fruit Salads, cricket stumps on the wall.
Goal posts were painted on solid red brick,
The game: knock down ginger, that annoying old trick.
No car, no heating, no fridge, melted butter,
Sixpence an iced Jubbly that always fell in the gutter.

Sherbert Lemons • Rhubarb & Custard • Gobstoppers • Pear Drops • Pontefract Cakes
Liquorice Comfits • Liquorice Sticks • Black Jacks • Fruit Salads

Saturday morning pictures, you've flown with The Few,
Leave the cinema by twelve, shooting bandits at two.
Bob Danvers-Walker on Movietone News,
'With our boys in the air we just couldn't lose.'
You're a Lancaster Bomber, you're a Messerschmitt plane,
You're *The Spirit of Kent* all over again.
Shot down by the wood yard, you cry 'it's not fair',
You fly home to Mum on a wing and a prayer.

The coalman and milkman delivered by horse,
With Granddad behind them...for the roses of course.
Golliwogs on jam pots, Black and White Minstrels on telly,
No politically correct with a backbone of jelly.
An orange box go-cart with the wheels off a pram,
Getting your bike stuck in the lines of the tram.
School pens with nibs that you dipped in the ink,
Those glorious days when the world map was pink.

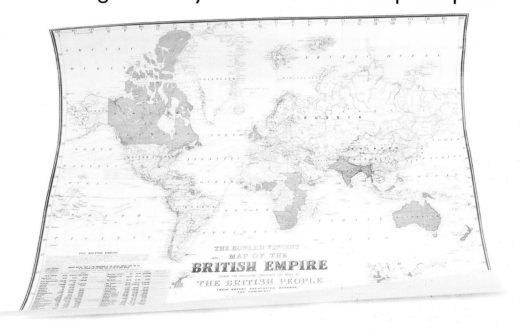

'All Things Bright and Beautiful', I remember it well,
The assembly hall, that sweaty-feet smell.
Miss Walker my first teacher, the boy who had fits,
The young PE mistress with enormous great tits.
The lessons that taught us that Britain IS Great,
Nowadays that's something New Labour would hate.
The summers seemed longer, the roads they did melt,
The girl in 3C, my God how she smelt.

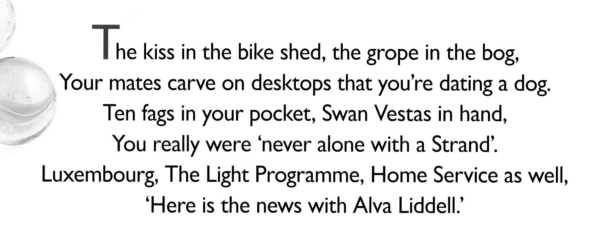

The kiss in the bike shed, the grope in the bog,
Your mates carve on desktops that you're dating a dog.
Ten fags in your pocket, Swan Vestas in hand,
You really were 'never alone with a Strand'.
Luxembourg, The Light Programme, Home Service as well,
'Here is the news with Alva Liddell.'

21

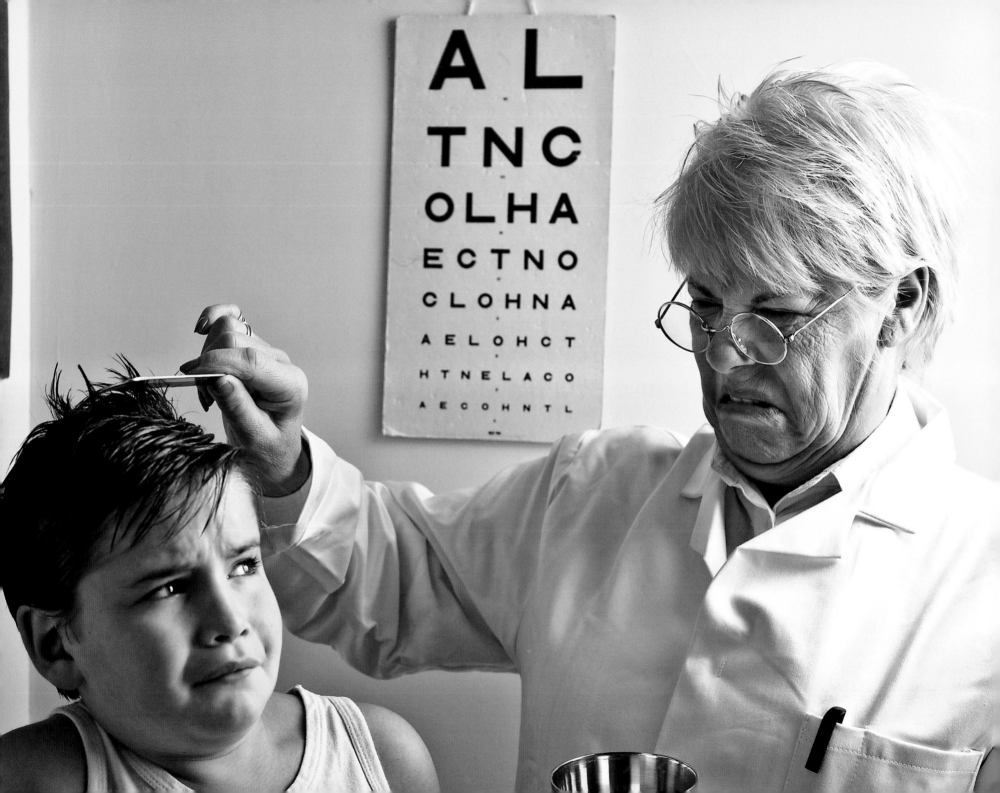

The women in white coats, metal combs in their hands,
Searching your hair, every last strand.
Standing in line, your legs all akimbo,
Your balls in the hand of the ugly old bimbo,
You gaze to heaven, she asks you to cough,
You hope and you pray that nothing drops off.
You gaze at the young nurse, her perfume you whiff,
Suddenly a part of you starts to go stiff.
The old bimbo she smiles, she thinks she did the trick,
The headmaster's wooden ruler lands on your dick.

Grazed knees full of gravel, a swing in the park,
The ghost in the outside lav after dark.
Thick frost on the windows, not outside but in,
The first bus conductor with chocolate skin.
The constable's cape round the back of your head,
'What you doin' 'ere son? Should be tucked up in bed.'

Pineapple Chunks in the sweetshop, Cough Candies and all,
You'd kill your best friend for an Aniseed Ball.
Lead soldiers, tin cars, Meccano sets with a spanner,
A Red Rover round London for two and a tanner.
Dogs stuck together, cold water you throw,
A hard lump of darning that blisters your toe.

29

'CORONA' FAMI DRIN

LONDON TRANSPORT

G350 BN 162 G350

U.W. 7 10 0
SPEED:~30 M.P.H.

LONDON PASSENGER TRANSPORT BOARD
55 BROADWAY
WESTMINSTER, S.W.I.

A dogfight with a Corgi or Dinky Toy held high,
You cripple the Gerry, then land for Mum's pie.
Powdered mustard, Dolly clothes dye, gypsies with pegs,
Those horrible short trousers that chaffed both your legs.
Patted butter from Sainsbury's, luncheon meat, Spam,
Used, snotty hankies boiling up in a pan.
Local picture palace, matinee flicks,
Dorothy Wilson showed us her knicks.

The showers after football, the boy well endowed,
Hanging our boots on his knob drew a crowd.
The screams from the changing rooms, girls in a stew,
The hole in the wall, your best part poking through.
Bunking off school, 'hopping the wag',
A cigarette with a pin in for that very last drag.

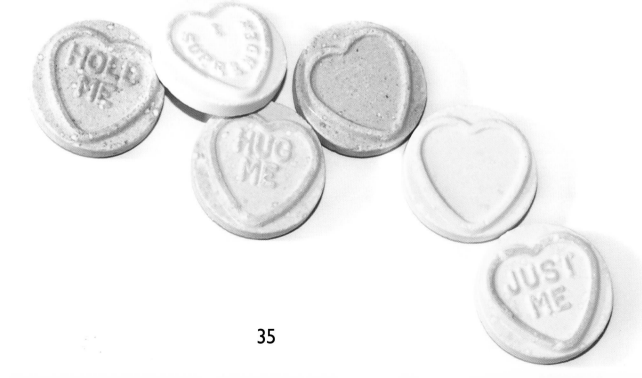

Dad's in the doghouse, the pub's got the rent,
Navy-blue knickers the size of a tent.
A fart in assembly, six of the best,
Getting a suntan the shape of your vest.
A Cisco kid watch, a present for me,
Spitting a 'greeny' in the headmaster's tea.

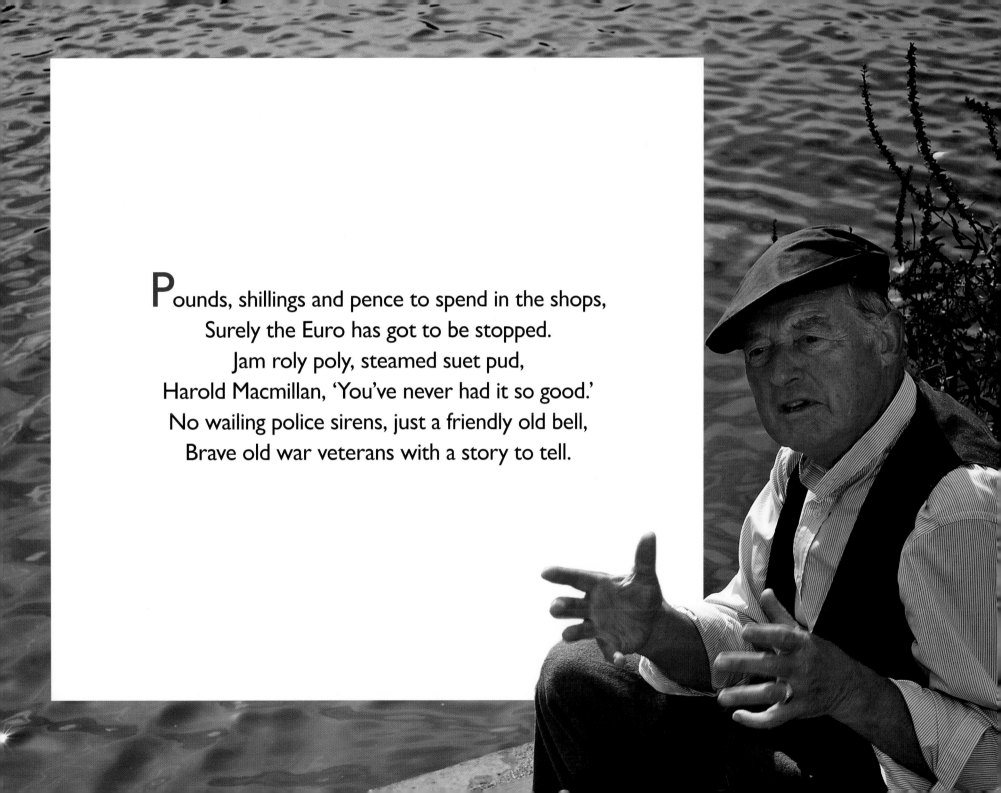

Pounds, shillings and pence to spend in the shops,
Surely the Euro has got to be stopped.
Jam roly poly, steamed suet pud,
Harold Macmillan, 'You've never had it so good.'
No wailing police sirens, just a friendly old bell,
Brave old war veterans with a story to tell.

THRILLING NEW

FOURPENCE-HALFPENNY

EVERY WE

EAGL

22 OCTOBER 1954 Vol. 5

THE STO
Believing th
when th

The Beano, *The Dandy, Eagle* comic I read,
Fighting the Mekon alone in your bed.
Hopalong Cassidy, Lone Ranger, The Cisco Kid,
Did John Wayne get shot? 'The hell he did.'
Sink the Bismarck!, Dambusters, The Longest Day,
We showed those Germans, we *were* playing away.

Back then there was only one car in the street,
The place where the cowboys and Indians would meet.
When the caps in the Lone Star guns shot you dead,
With your bow and your arrow, *your* Indian was red.
Planning to ambush Flo Spreadbury was fun,
Usually finished up with a belting for son.
You rode into town in your ten gallon hat,
On your three-wheeled horse you *so* proudly sat.

Arthur Askey, Frankie Howerd, 'Don't, Missus' he'd sing,
Dear old Max Miller, 'Now here's a funny thing.'
Jelly Babies by the quarter from our local store,
Ask for the boy ones 'cos you always get more.
Tuppence is all it cost us to travel by bus,
'One more inside, are you travellin' wid us?'

Teddy Boys on street corners in their drainpipe suits,
Spud guns, peashooters, cap bombs to boot.
A Dansette record player, Buddy Holly's lost plane,
The flash of a stocking top now and again.
Everley Brothers sang hits like 'Here Comes Cathy's Clown',
Our parents would shout, 'Turn that racket down.'

This rhyme could go on, there's five decades to go,
But I'd finish as old as my dear Uncle Joe.
So for those who remember, the times they were tough,
But love and affection? There was more than enough.
As we re-live these memories, it was fun through and through,
It just leaves me to say... Thanks, to The Few.

They Did It For You

That he may run, that he may play, they reached for the sky day after day.
In their Spitfires, their Hurricanes, with Bomber Command,
In defence of us all without order or demand.
Seventy years ago those boys, some barely out of school,
Sacrificed a whole lifetime for the sake of us all.
The wailing sirens to scramble, there was little relent,
But those boys did us proud in the skies over Kent.

The 'pop, pop' of propellers that build to a roar,
A farewell to your dog, will you see him once more?
The crackle of the radio, the taste of the fuel,
Passing thoughts of a loved one, the timing so cruel.
Flight checks in a cockpit the size of your shoe,
Your veins open wide as adrenalin pumps through.
The chocks are removed, your bird's in the air,
The throttle wide open, it's no ride at the fair.

The pull on the joystick, she climbs out of sight,
You join the formation, your pals left and right.
Your wits are about you, you share eyes and ears,
Look after each other or it'll all end in tears.
The drone of the engines, that soporific sound,
Fighting sleep every second 5,000 feet from the ground.
The silence is broken, the crackling radio shouts,
'Bandits at six o'clock, for Christ's sake look out.'

You realise a Messerschmitt is terrifyingly near,
You recognise that smell, the smell of pure fear.
The 'rat-a-tat' of his guns, shells fly past your head,
In confusion you really don't know if you're dead.
'There's no blood, I'm still breathing, still flying my plane,'
Your mind plays this thought over and over again.
You're in the grip of a dogfight, the English Channel below,
'Please tell my mum, I really want her to know.'

It's worse than imagined, far worse without fail,
The Luftwaffe Messerschmitt is still on your tail,
Thank God for your Spitfire, you throw it into a dive,
'Don't think much of my chances of getting home alive.'
Another pull on the joystick, just feet from the sea,
'Now I'm chasing the bastard, he's not chasing me.'
Your guns all a-blazing, a continuous stream,
The enemy goes down with that tell-tale last scream.

'He's the enemy I hate him, someone's son, someone's dad.'
You know this is war, but the killing feels bad.
Miles away you can feel it, a family's sad loss,
You pass the blame on to Hitler, just showing him who's boss.
Mawkish thoughts brushed aside as smoke fills your plane,
'Jesus Christ I'm on fire, will I see Mum again?'
The heat so intense, 'God the pain, Christ the stink,'
To stop your flesh burning, you ditch your crate in the drink.

They sent two thousand six hundred Luftwaffe planes,
Just six hundred and forty fought back in our name.
With courage, tenacity, against formidable foe,
They took their lives in their hands for the folk down below.
They had wives, they had sweethearts, mums full of tears,
'Killed or Missing In Action' was each one of their fears.
They lost friends, they lost brothers, a pint stands un-drunk,
Planes ditched in the Channel, their trapped bodies sunk.

There was young Ernest Salaway just twenty two,
A gunner on a Halifax with the rest, a young crew.
So proud was Ernest, flying the first 'Thousand Bomber Raid'.
But our young gunner, the hero, with his life dearly paid.
Flying over Holland at fifteen thousand feet,
'F' for Freddie was hit, the outlook quite bleak.

They plummeted through the intense cold of the night,
Not a thought for the bravery, no time for the fright.
Sergeant Smith pulled the D-ring on his parachute pack.
Two lives were at stake, there was no going back.
As the silk canopy deployed with that reassuring rip,
Ernest couldn't hold on, his numbed fingers lost grip.

Sergeant Smith, full of horror had to watch his friend go,
Out of sight, through the darkness, towards the ground far below.
Ernest Salaway's body of just twenty-two years,
Lay lifeless, sadly crumpled, for his family just tears.
So be mindful of Ernest, losing grip of his mate,
For his pain and his sacrifice was truly quite great.

You probably weren't born when so many men died,
It was your lifetime of freedom they set out to decide.
They lost sleep, they lost minds, they lost limbs, they lost life.
For your freedom was balanced on the edge of a knife.
The Battle of Britain was raging, four months in the air,
Give thanks to the heroes who fought for you there.

'We don't want to be remembered as heroes,' they said.
Just remember their words as you sleep safe in your bed.
They regarded it as 'a privilege to fight for freedom, fair play',
Just remember their words as you go about your day.
They won't appear on *EastEnders* or on *X Factor* sing,
But they're real celebrities, for your freedom they bring.

When you read of these heroes,
and how some of them died,
Always purchase your poppy, and wear it with pride.
Seventy years, a distant memory, secured freedom for you.
For the life you live now? Give thanks to 'The Few'.
'Never was so much owed by so many to so few',
Winston Churchill was right you know, yes, they did it for you.

with THANKS to

Peter Monk, for the use of his wonderful Spitfire. This magnificent aircraft based at Biggin Hill in Kent is available for films/TV/photoshoots/displays. Contact Peter on www.kentspitfire.co.uk

www.aquarterof.co.uk
Over 700 varieties of traditional sweets including old favourites like Wham bars, Anglo Bubbly, Black Jacks, Chelsea Whoppers, fizzy cola bottles and Flying Saucers. The website instantly transports you back to your childhood, complete with good old-fashioned service.

Tony Lay and The Cobham London Bus Museum. The largest collection of old London buses in the world. Most of the preserved vehicles are in operational condition and are available for films/TV/photoshoots/commemorative days. Visitors to the museum can experience travel from a bygone era. For all the information you need, visit their website www.londonbusmuseum.com

Colin Pocknell for the use of his classic 1952 Humber Hawk. This remarkable car, in its original condition, is available for hire from pockers222@hotmail.co.uk

Foxtrot Productions Ltd, supplier of costume, uniform and insignia. Telephone 0208 964 3555.